Photo·Guide to the NEW TESTAMENT

LION PUBLISHING

Lion Publishing
29-33 Lower Kings Rd
Berkhamsted, Herts, UK

Photographs and notes by
David Alexander

Bible quotations from the Revised Standard Version,
copyright 1946 and 1952 by the Division of
Christian Education, National Council of the
Churches of Christ, USA

First edition September 1972

International Standard Book Number 0 85648 001 0

Printed in Great Britain by
Purnell and Sons Ltd, Paulton

Introduction

Those who have been to the sites of the New Testament story, in Israel and Jordan, Greece and Turkey, will know the excitement of seeing the places where the events actually took place. It makes the Bible events come to life. It helps us understand the text of the New Testament afresh. The aim of this book is the same; to provide pictures which make the setting of the New Testament live for those who cannot visit the places themselves.

It often comes as a surprise to the visitor to the Middle East to find so many remains from New Testament times. There is no reason why there should be this surprise, for the Bible consists of documents which are at least as trust-worthy historically as any ancient writings. But each year sees some new attack on the Bible's reliability (usually by people who do not want it to be true because they do not dare to face the challenge of its message). So it still comes as a confirmation to faith when people find its setting so obviously and accurately that of the Jewish, Roman and Hellenistic world which has left so many traces for us to see and admire.

In fact the person looking for New Testament sites often finds himself on the main tourist track. Places such as Ephesus in Western Turkey not only provide a marvellous aid to under-standing the drama of the New Testament Acts and Epistles but are also among the main attractions of the area for those who have no prior interest in the Bible. This serves to underline the fact that the events of the New Testament which so determined the subsequent history, culture and hope of the civilized world took place at a unique time in history. Hebrew religion, Greek language and culture, Roman imperial administration made possible the immediate and widespread dissemination of the Christian good news. No wonder St Paul maintained that 'the time had fully come'. The time was ripe in a way which it has never been before or since.

The choice of pictures has been determined by the aim of the book. Thus some of the traditional sites have not been included, although they have been hallowed by centuries of devotion, because they no longer help us to imagine what it must have been like in New Testament times. The picture of a first-century tomb complete with rolling stone is quite simply more informative and more evocative than a picture of the church built on the traditional site of Jesus' burial. A photograph of the Roman pavement where Jesus actually stood trial before Pilate has been chosen as more suitable for this particular purpose than, say, one which shows the Stations of the Cross.

The aim of this book, then, is not only simple; it is practical. It is intended to help ordinary people understand the Bible all the better for seeing it against its background, and to remind them that it is not a fairy story to be grown out of, but the record of what actually happened over nineteen hundred years ago in Mediterranean towns and countryside which can still be seen.

The Bible is historical. But it is more than that. It is meant to take us beyond the background, which can be conjured up with the help of a book such as this, to the Person who is at the centre of the picture. He has not changed. He is alive today, and as relevant as when the message of his forgiveness, power and challenge revolutionized the ancient world. It is hoped that the stimulus of these photographs and brief accompanying comment will make many turn afresh to read the New Testament itself with a new confidence in its historicity and a new willingness to hear its message.

Michael Green
*St John's College,
Nottingham*

Contents

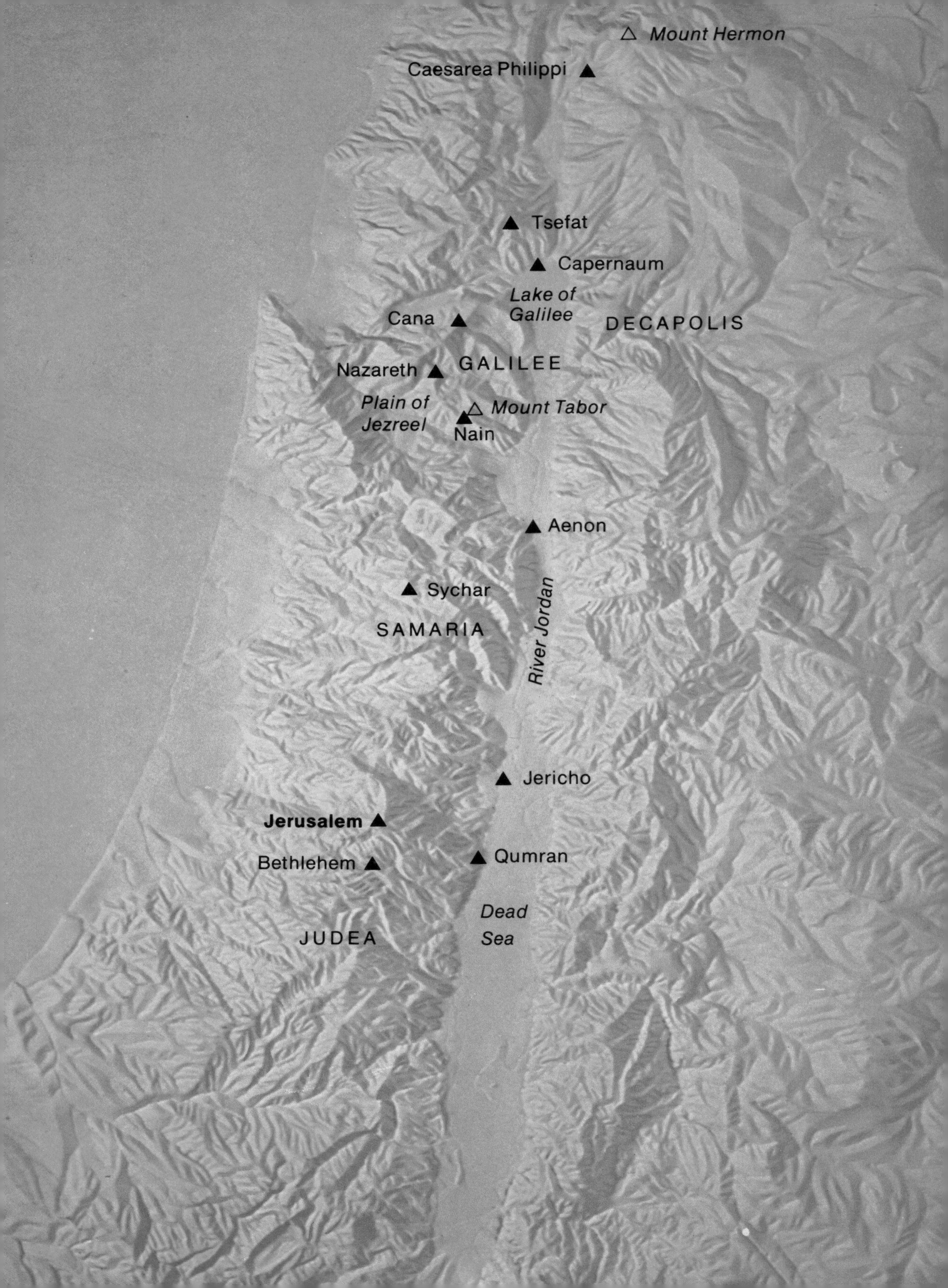

△ *Mount Hermon*

Caesarea Philippi ▲

▲ Tsefat

▲ Capernaum

Lake of Galilee

Cana ▲

DECAPOLIS

Nazareth ▲ GALILEE

Plain of Jezreel △ *Mount Tabor*
▲
Nain

▲ Aenon

▲ Sychar

River Jordan

SAMARIA

▲ Jericho

Jerusalem ▲

Bethlehem ▲ ▲ Qumran

Dead Sea

JUDEA

PART ONE

The Life
and Teaching
of Jesus

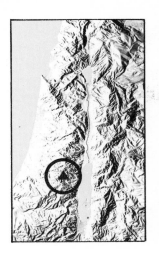

Bethlehem

'In those days a decree went out from Caesar Augustus that all the world should be enrolled . . . And Joseph also went up from Galilee, from the city of Nazareth, to Judea, to the city of David, which is called Bethlehem, because he was of the house and lineage of David, to be enrolled with Mary, his betrothed, who was with child. And while they were there, the time came for her to be delivered. And she gave birth to her first-born son . . .' Luke 2: 1-7

Bethlehem stands on a ridge on the edge of the arid Judean desert, just south of Jerusalem. It is still surrounded by fields, with shepherds 'watching their flocks', as when Jesus was born. The Emperor Augustus was not to know that his decree would bring Joseph and Mary down to Bethlehem and so fulfil the prophet Micah's prediction that it would be from Bethlehem that a ruler would come 'who will govern my people Israel'.

Nazareth

'They returned into Galilee, to their own city, Nazareth. And the child grew and became strong, filled with wisdom; and the favour of God was upon him.'
Luke 2: 39, 40

Up the steep escarpment from the broad Plain of Jezreel, Nazareth lies cupped in the hills of Galilee, 1230 ft above sea level. Today Nazareth is a town with a sizeable population. But before it became the home of Jesus it was little known: it is not mentioned at all in the Old Testament. And though in New Testament times it was a busy town near the cross-roads of the Roman trade-routes, it still called forth the comment, 'Can anything good come out of Nazareth?' (John 1: 46).

Aenon near Salim

'John was baptizing at Aenon near Salim, because there was much water there; and people came and were baptized.' John 3:23

John the Baptist called people to turn from evil because 'the kingdom was at hand' — to shed their sin, like dead leaves and undergo the public 'washing' of baptism. In a country where water is sparse it was natural that his activity should be concentrated in the Jordan valley. Here the valley is already well below sea level, the heat and humidity producing sub-tropical vegetation.

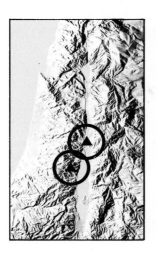

River Jordan

'Then Jesus came from Galilee to the Jordan to John, to be baptized by him. John would have prevented him, saying, "I need to be baptized by you, and do you come to me?" But Jesus answered him, "Let it be so now; for thus it is fitting for us to fulfil all righteousness." '
Matthew 3: 13-15

The Jordan river rises at the foot of Mount Hermon on the border with Lebanon and Syria. After the Lake of Galilee it winds down through dense scrub and thickets towards the Dead Sea. It is not a large or pretentious river — in Old Testament days Naaman, the Syrian general, was quite indignant when Elisha told him to wash in it. But it was in this river that Jesus identified himself with the sins of his people as he allowed himself to be baptized.

The Judean desert

'Then Jesus was led up by the Spirit into the wilderness to be tempted by the devil. And he fasted forty days and forty nights, and afterward he was hungry. And the tempter came and said to him, "If you are the Son of God, command these stones to become loaves of bread" . . .' Matthew 4

It was somewhere in this arid, stony desert south of Jerusalem that Jesus faced in advance the temptations that would threaten his whole ministry. He answered his tempter in words which go back to the testing of the children of Israel during their forty years in the wilderness centuries before, 'Man shall not live by bread alone . . .'

'Then the devil took him to the holy city, and set him on the pinnacle of the temple . . .' The great south-east corner of the temple area was the vivid setting for Jesus' next temptation. 'If you are the Son of God, throw yourself down . . .' (Matthew 4: 5, 6).

17

Galilee fishing-boats

'Passing along by the Sea of Galilee, he saw Simon and Andrew the brother of Simon casting a net in the sea; for they were fishermen. And Jesus said to them, "Follow me and I will make you become fishers of men." And immediately they left their nets and followed him. And going on a little farther, he saw James the son of Zebedee and John his brother, who were in their boat mending the nets. And immediately he called them . . .'
Mark 1: 16-20

The Galilee fishing industry was a sizeable one in New Testament times. The fish was dried and taken to Jerusalem (via the 'Fish Gate'). John's detailed knowledge of Jerusalem suggests that the family business may have had a 'city office' there. A reference in Pliny to the fish pickled at Tarichaea by Galilee shows that it was exported throughout the Mediterranean world.

Cana in Galilee

'There was a marriage at Cana in Galilee, and the mother of Jesus was there; Jesus also was invited to the marriage, with his disciples . . .'
John 2: 1, 2

The name 'Cana' is preserved in the present-day village of Kafr Kana, a few miles east of Nazareth in the Galilean hills. John selects the wedding where Jesus turned water into wine as the first of the 'signs' in his Gospel. The water was for 'the Jewish rites of purification': Jesus had come to bring the wine of the new age, the gospel.

Villagers still come to the well in Kafr Kana to draw water.

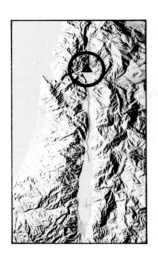

Capernaum

'And they went into Capernaum; and immediately on the sabbath he entered the synagogue and taught. And they were astonished at his teaching, for he taught them as one who had authority, and not as the scribes.' Mark 1: 21, 22

Capernaum was Jesus' base for much of his teaching and healing ministry in Galilee. It was the home town of Peter and Andrew. It was also the place where the Roman centurion whose slave was healed by Jesus had built a synagogue (Luke 7: 5). The ruin of the synagogue on the site of Capernaum dates from the second century, but it shows the same combination of Roman architecture with Jewish symbolism that would also have characterized the earlier one.

The palm, a symbol of the land of Israel, carved on the synagogue stone-work.

More Jewish symbols: a bunch of grapes and a star.

Galilee countryside

'He went on through cities and villages, preaching and bringing the good news of the kingdom of God. And the twelve were with him . . .' Luke 8: 1

Behind the hills which flank the edge of the Plain of Jezreel lies Nazareth. The village in the foreground is at the foot of Mount Tabor. In New Testament times Galilee was at the intersection of important trade-routes: Jesus' teaching was in no backwater but in a busy, if second-class, province of the Roman Empire.

Known as the 'Mount of Precipitation' this rocky hill is just near Nazareth. It might well have been where Jesus was taken when the outraged inhabitants of Nazareth threatened to 'throw him down headlong'. The claims of Jesus were too much for the people of his own home town.

City on a hill

'A city on a hill cannot be hid. Nor do men light a lamp and put it under a bushel, but on a stand, and it gives light to all in the house. Let your light so shine before men, that they may see your good works and give glory to your Father who is in heaven.' Matthew 5:14-16

Much of the teaching of Jesus was in the form of object-lessons and parables from life around. The 'city on a hill' pictured here is Tsefat in Upper Galilee, for long a centre of Jewish learning and devotion.

Oil-lamps typical of the very many found from Roman and later periods (Archaeological Museum, Istanbul)

'Beware of practising your piety before men' (Matthew 6:1)

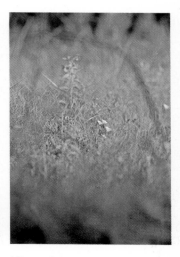

'Consider the lilies of the field, how they grow . . .' (Matthew 6:28)

Jacob's well

'So he came to a city of Samaria, called Sychar, near the field that Jacob gave to his son Joseph. Jacob's well was there, and so Jesus, wearied as he was with his journey, sat down beside the well. It was about the sixth hour. There came a woman of Samaria to draw water . . .' John 4:5-7

This well is typical of those still in use in country areas. Not only racial prejudice (verse 9) but also the fact that women were despised (verse 27) made it surprising that Jesus stopped to talk to the woman of Samaria. But the result was a vital conversation: 'Whoever drinks of the water I shall give shall never thirst . . .'

Jacob's well itself is now enclosed within a church; it is still true that 'the well is deep'; and the water is as good as when Jacob first dug it.

The Good Shepherd

'. . . The sheep hear his voice, and he calls his own sheep by name and leads them out . . . He goes before them, and the sheep follow him, for they know his voice . . . I am the good shepherd.'
John 10:3, 4, 11

Traditionally the Eastern shepherd would not drive his sheep but lead them. When several flocks were mixed they could be separated simply by the shepherd's call to his own sheep. At night when they were in a sheepfold of rocks and stone walls the shepherd would lie across the door to protect them: he was also the 'door of the sheep'.

Nain

'Soon afterward he went to a city called Nain, and his disciples and a great crowd went with him. As he drew near to the gate of the city, behold, a man who had died was being carried out, the only son of his mother, and she was a widow . . . And when the Lord saw her, he had compassion on her . . .' Luke 7:11-13

A village on the slope of a hill looking towards the rounded hump of Mt Tabor, Nain was the scene of the demonstration of the power of Jesus over death itself.

Storm over the lake

'Leaving the crowd, they took him with them, just as he was, in the boat. And other boats were with him. And a great storm of wind arose . . . And he awoke and rebuked the wind, and said to the sea, "Peace! Be still! . . ." Mark 4:36-39

Jesus claimed power not only over sickness and death itself, but also over creation: 'Who then is this, that even wind and sea obey him?' (verse 41). Fishing boats used on the Lake of Galilee are small; and a storm can soon blot out the coast-line and raise a heavy sea.

Lake of Galilee

'He made the disciples get into the boat and go before him to the other side, while he dismissed the crowds . . .' Matthew 14:22

Jesus used the lake as an escape-route from the crowds. He taught the people on the beach from a boat. The lake was used to teach his disciples faith. This view is of the north-western corner of it, looking from near Tiberias toward the site of Magdala and Gennesaret.

The sower

'And he told them many things in parables, saying: "A sower went out to sow. And as he sowed, some seeds fell along the path, and the birds came and devoured them. Other seeds fell on rocky ground, . . . upon thorns, . . . on good soil . . ."' Matthew 13:3-8

Jesus spoke in parables, using everyday examples to get his message across. But he also used parables to appeal to people's will as much as to their understanding: only people who really wanted to follow him would grasp the meaning, not the wilfully blind or those who had no intention of obeying (Matthew 13:10-17). The picture of the 'soils' was taken in Galilee; Mt Moreh is in the background.

The Good Samaritan

'A man was going down from Jerusalem to Jericho, and he fell among robbers, who stripped him and beat him, and departed, leaving him half-dead . . .' Luke 10:30

Jesus' story of the man who was beaten up on the Jericho road would have been only too real to his hearers in Jerusalem. The road passes through rocky, desert country as it winds down to Jericho in the Jordan valley. The ruin of an inn still stands where an inn has stood for centuries. But the twist in the story may not have proved so easy to accept: it was a despised Samaritan, not the religious people, who showed true love for his neighbour.

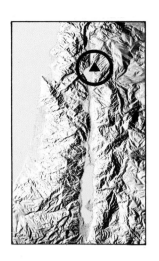

Lakeside miracles

'They came to the other side of the sea, to the country of the Gerasenes (or Gadarenes). And when he had come out of the boat, there met him out of the tombs a man with an unclean spirit . . . And the unclean spirits came out, and entered the swine; and the herd, numbering about two thousand, rushed down the steep bank into the sea . . .' Mark 5:1-13

The district of Gerasa, Gadara and Gergesa was east of the Lake of Galilee, an area known for its 'ten towns', or decapolis, occupied by Greeks: this would explain why there was so large a herd of swine, for pork was a forbidden food for the Jew. The picture looks toward the north-eastern end of the lake.

It was at the north-east end of the lake, too, that a crowd of five thousand were fed from five loaves and two small fishes. These fish are known today as 'St Peter's Fish' because of their large mouth (in which they carry their eggs); see Matthew 17:27. The fish in the story of the feeding of the five thousand may well, however, have been pickled, or salted, rather than fresh.

44

Caesarea Philippi

'Now when Jesus came into the district of Caesarea Philippi, he asked the disciples, "Who do men say that the Son of Man is?" . . . Simon Peter replied, "You are the Christ, the Son of the living God." And Jesus answered him, ". . . you are Peter, and on this rock I will build my church . . ."' Matthew 16:2, 6

Caesarea Philippi was built by the tetrarch Philip (son of Herod the Great) and dedicated to 'Caesar', the Roman Emperor. It was formerly known as Paneas, derived from the veneration of the Great God Pan. So it was against the background both of Emperor-worship and 'pantheism' that Peter made his confession; and against the background of a rock cliff which dominates one of the sources of the Jordan.

Mount Hermon

'Jesus took with him Peter and James and John his brother, and led them up a high mountain apart. And he was transfigured before them, and his face shone like the sun, and his garments became white as light . . . and a voice from the cloud said, "This is my beloved Son, with whom I am well pleased; listen to him."' Matthew 17:1, 2, 5

Mount Hermon is very near Caesarea Philippi, and so it has long been supposed that this mountain was the site of the transfiguration. It is certainly a 'high mountain', rising to 9,100 ft, and dominating Upper Galilee. The picture is of dawn over Mt Hermon.

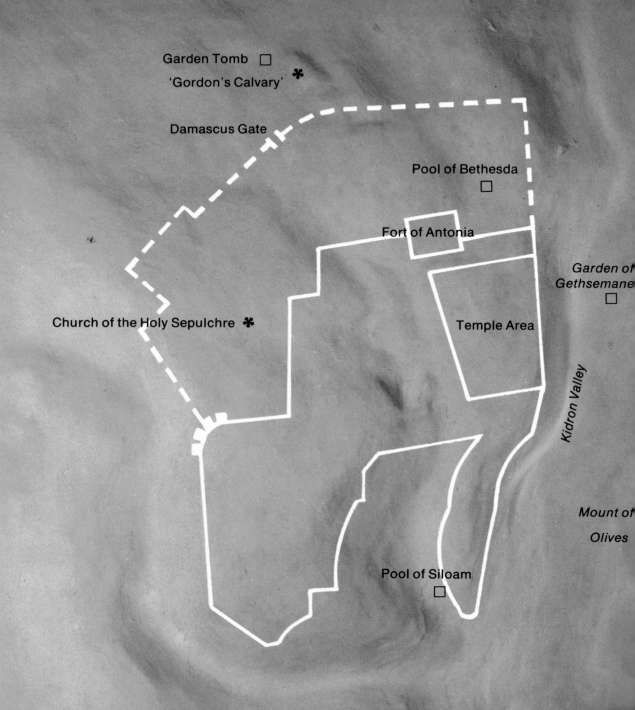

Garden Tomb □
'Gordon's Calvary' ✳

Damascus Gate

Pool of Bethesda
□

Fort of Antonia

Garden of
Gethsemane
□

Church of the Holy Sepulchre ✳

Temple Area

Kidron Valley

Mount of
Olives

Pool of Siloam
□

Bethany

PART TWO

Opposition and Triumph

Synagogue

'He entered the synagogue, and a man was there who had a withered hand. And they watched him, to see whether he would heal him on the sabbath, so that they might accuse him.' Mark 3:1, 2

From the beginning of his ministry Jesus taught in the Jewish synagogues. But the religious leaders who had reduced the law to a tyranny of petty rules strongly resented every move he made to restore the true meaning of God's law.

Another synagogue: both are in Tsefat, in Galilee.

An orthodox Jew with a phylactery — passages from the law in a small box — bound to his forehead in literal obedience to commandments such as Deuteronomy 6:8.

The clash with orthodoxy

'Then Pharisees and scribes came to Jesus from Jerusalem and said, "Why do your disciples transgress the tradition of the elders? For they do not wash their hands when they eat." He answered them, "And why do you transgress the commandment of God for the sake of your tradition? . . ."'
Matthew 15:1-3

In such places as Tsefat, pictured here, and the Mea Shearim quarter of Jerusalem today, ultra-orthodox Jews seek to live out the minutiae of the observance of the law and rabbinic traditions.

Those who led 'little ones' astray were fit only to have a mill-stone tied round their necks and be cast into the sea.

Jesus compared the Pharisees to 'whited sepulchres', tombs whitewashed outside but rotten inside.

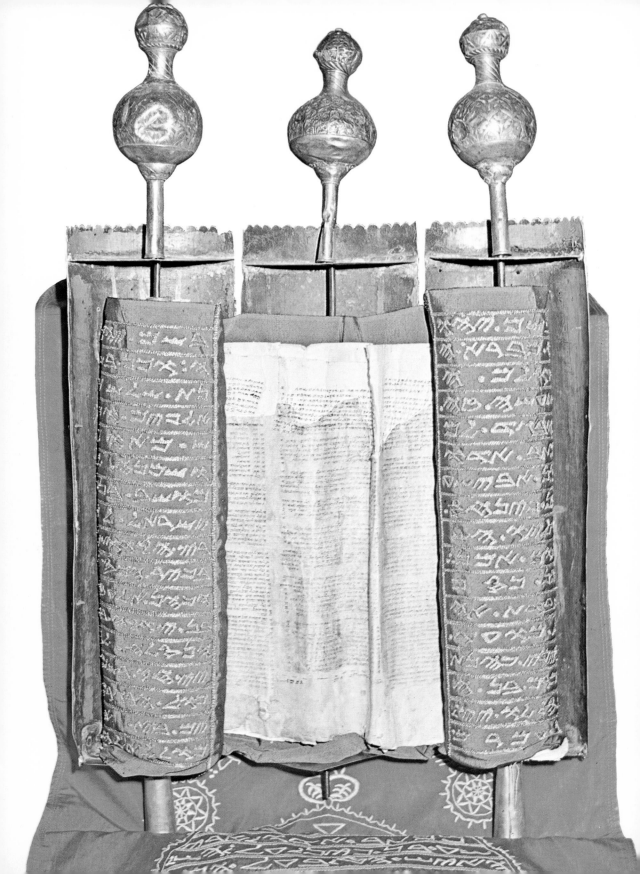

The law

'Think not that I have come to abolish the law and the prophets; I have not come to abolish them but to fulfil them. For truly, I say to you, till heaven and earth pass away, not an iota, not a dot, will pass from the law until all is accomplished.' Matthew 5:17, 18

This ancient scroll of the Pentateuch, the first five books of the Bible, belongs to the Samaritan synagogue in Nablus, near ancient Shechem.

An orthodox Jew studying the law.

Jerusalem

'O Jerusalem, Jerusalem, killing the prophets and stoning those who are sent to you! How often would I have gathered your children together as a hen gathers her brood under her wings, and you would not! . . .' Luke 13:34.

The Old City of Jerusalem is enclosed by walls dating back to medieval times. It is a square-shaped maze of narrow streets and ancient buildings. The more modern buildings of the new Jerusalem rise behind. The gate is known as St Stephen's Gate after the first Christian martyr—whose death was a grim confirmation of Jesus' lament over the city.

57

The Pool of Bethesda

'Now there is in Jerusalem by the sheep gate a pool, in Hebrew called Beth-zatha (or Bethesda), which has five porticoes. In these lay a multitude of invalids, blind, lame, paralyzed. One man was there who had been ill for thirty-eight years . . . Jesus said to him, "Rise, take up your pallet, and walk." . . .' John 5:2-5, 8

Archaeologists discovered, deep below the present level of Jerusalem, a pool with five porticoes . . . Mixed with remains from Crusader times there is stonework going back to the time of Jesus himself, and earlier.

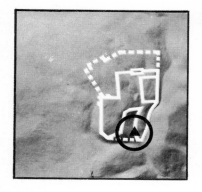

The Pool of Siloam is associated with another miracle of Jesus in Jerusalem: the healing of the man blind from birth (John 9). It goes back to the engineering feat of Hezekiah about 700 BC, when a rock tunnel 1,700 ft long was dug to bring water inside the city from a spring outside.

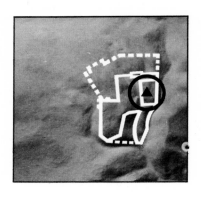

The temple area

'And every day he was teaching in the temple, but at night he went out and lodged on the mount called Olivet. And early in the morning all the people came to him in the temple to hear him.'
Luke 21:37, 38

The large temple area, formerly resplendent with courts and porticoes, is now almost bare except for two large mosques. The golden-domed Mosque of Omar stands over the rock of Mount Moriah, where Abraham showed his willingness to sacrifice his son Isaac. It was in the courtyards of the temple that the money-changers and sellers of 'official' sacrifices were fleecing the poor. Teachers would gather their disciples around them in the Temple porticoes. Here too the early church met. 'They were all together in Solomon's Portico' (Acts 5:12).

Inscription in Greek forbidding Gentiles on pain of death to enter the temple precincts (see Acts 21:28) (Istanbul Archaeological Museum).

Teaching on the end

'But when you see Jerusalem surrounded by armies, then know that its desolation has come near. Then let those who are in Judea flee to the mountains . . .'
Luke 21:20, 21

In the course of his teaching on the final events up to the end of time Jesus dramatically foretold the destruction of Jerusalem—which happened some forty years later in AD 70. In a relief on the Titus Arch in Rome, plunder from the Temple of Jerusalem is seen being carried in triumph by the victorious Romans.

In 1947 the Dead Sea Scrolls, manuscripts of Old Testament books, were discovered in a cave, untouched since they had been hidden there before the Roman army over-ran the area in AD 68. Nearby are the remains of Qumran, the settlement of a monastic Jewish community which owned the manuscripts: there are clear evidences of violent destruction in the ruins.

Jerusalem street

'Some of the people of Jerusalem therefore said, "Is not this the man whom they seek to kill? And here he is, speaking openly, and they say nothing to him! Can it be that the authorities really know that this is the Christ? . . . When the Christ appears, will he do more signs than this man has done?" The Pharisees heard the crowd thus muttering about him, and the chief priests and Pharisees sent officers to arrest him.' John 7:25, 26, 31, 32

In the tangle of crowded narrow streets in the old city of Jerusalem it is easy to imagine the rumour and intrigue which surrounded the last days of the ministry of Jesus. The conflict with the religious leaders was coming to a head. The city was full of pilgrims, in Jerusalem for the Festival of the Passover. Tension was at breaking-point.

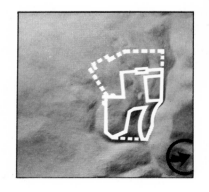

The nearby village of Bethany offered Jesus a refuge away from the crowded city. It was the home of Martha, Mary and Lazarus — and the scene of one of Jesus' most striking miracles (John 11).

The vine

'I am the vine, you are the branches. He who abides in me, and I in him, he it is that bears much fruit, for apart from me you can do nothing. If a man does not abide in me, he is cast forth as a branch and withers . . .' John 15:5, 6

It was after the Last Supper, in the course of the Passover Feast, that Jesus taught his close disciples about their coming relationship to himself. Each branch of a vine grows directly from the main 'stock'. After the grapes are picked the branches are cut right back, nearly to the stock. For much of the year the stock grows round them—they 'abide' in the vine. Then the new branches grow out rapidly to bear fruit. Branches which do not bear fruit are cut off altogether: they are of no use for anything but to be burnt.

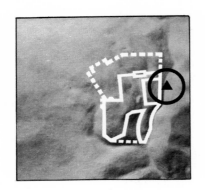

Gethsemane

'When Jesus had spoken these words, he went forth with his disciples across the Kidron valley, where there was a garden, which he and his disciples entered . . .'
John 18:1

Down from the walls of the old city, across a small valley, and up the slopes of the Mt of Olives opposite, there was a secluded garden where, John tells us, Jesus often met with his disciples. In the Garden of Gethsemane the tortured forms of these ancient olive trees, centuries old, still recall the agony which Jesus went through before his final arrest, as he faced the horror of a death in which he would be bearing the evil and alienation of human sin and separation from his Father.

The Pavement

'Then they led Jesus from the house of Caiaphas to the praetorium . . . Pilate sought to release him, but the Jews cried out, "If you release this man, you are not Caesar's friend; every one who makes himself a king sets himself against Caesar." When Pilate heard these words, he brought Jesus out and sat down on the judgment seat at a place called The Pavement, and in Hebrew, Gabbatha. . . . He said to the Jews, "Here is your King!" They cried out, "Away with him, away with him, crucify him!"' John 18:28; 19:12-15

The actual 'Pavement' of the Roman Fort of Antonia (the praetorium) was recently discovered under the Sisters of Zion Convent in Jerusalem. Scratched on some of the paving stones are the games the Roman soldiers once played. (This one is said to be for the ancient 'game of a king'. Traditionally the loser lost his life — it was a game often played with condemned prisoners. Kings would play it themselves — and if they lost have a slave put to death on their behalf.)

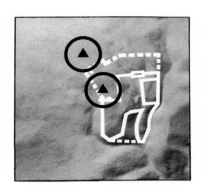

Place of a skull

'And they brought him to the place called Golgotha (which means the place of a skull). And they offered him wine mingled with myrrh; but he did not take it. And they crucified him, and divided his garments among them, casting lots for them, to decide what each should take. And it was the third hour, when they crucified him . . .' Mark 15:22-25

It is not certain precisely where Jesus was crucified. Traditionally it is on the site now marked by the Church of the Holy Sepulchre, which was formerly outside the city walls. Research on the location of the walls in New Testament times continues. It was General Gordon in the last century who suggested that this rocky outcrop outside the present northern wall bore a striking resemblance to the shape of a skull.

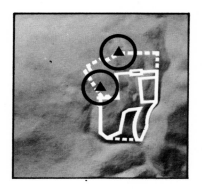

The empty tomb

'And when the sabbath was past, Mary Magdalene, and Mary the mother of James, and Salome, bought spices, so that they might go and anoint him. And very early on the first day of the week they went to the tomb when the sun had risen. And they were saying to one another, "Who will roll away the stone for us from the door of the tomb?" And looking up, they saw that the stone was rolled back; for it was very large . . .'
Mark 16:1-4

In an ancient garden just near 'Gordon's Calvary' outside the walls of Jerusalem is this tomb, a vivid example of the type in which Jesus was laid. A groove in front took the great stone which was rolled in front of the entrance.

Looking out from inside another first-century tomb, the stone in place by the entrance. This one was recently discovered in Nazareth beneath the Convent of the Sisters of Nazareth.

Inside, the body was 'bound in linen cloths with the spices' (John 19:40) and laid on a stone slab. When Peter came to the tomb of Jesus, 'he saw the linen cloths lying, and the napkin, which had been on his head, not lying with the linen cloths but rolled up in a place by itself. . . ' (John 20:6, 7). The body had gone, but the cloths had been left intact.

The great commission

'Now the eleven disciples went to Galilee, to the mountain to which Jesus had directed them. And when they saw him they worshipped him; but some doubted. And Jesus came and said to them, "All authority in heaven and earth has been given to me. Go therefore and make disciples of all nations . . ."'
Matthew 28:16-19

Looking towards the peaks of Mt Hermon in Upper Galilee.

Some of Jesus' resurrection appearances were in Jerusalem, some in Galilee. One took place on the shore of the Lake of Galilee, where the disciples had returned to their fishing. Jesus had prepared a fire on the beach and shared a breakfast of fish and bread with his disciples. Afterwards he gave to Peter, who had denied him three times, the opportunity to re-affirm three times his love for his Master. 'Jesus said to him, "Feed my sheep"' (John 21).

Ascension

' "You shall receive power when the Holy Spirit has come upon you; and you shall be my witnesses in Jerusalem and in all Judea and Samaria and to the end of the earth." And when he had said this, as they were looking on, he was lifted up, and a cloud took him out of their sight.'
Acts 1:8, 9

Luke also tells us where the ascension took place — on the Mount of Olives, the hill overlooking Jerusalem across the Kidron valley. (The tower is of a church commemorating the event.) And with the ascension came the promise that Jesus would come again.

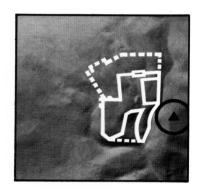

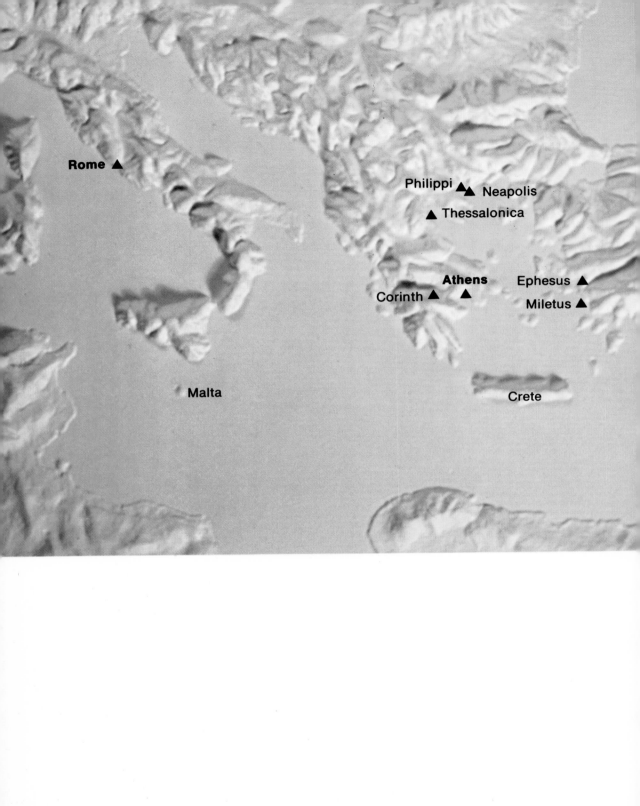

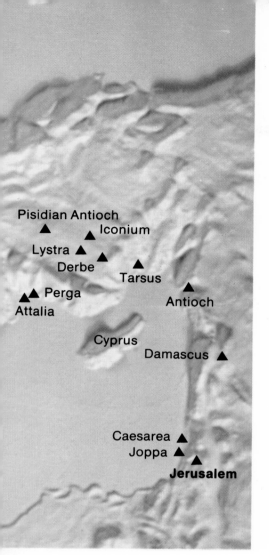

PART THREE

Outreach
of the
Early Church

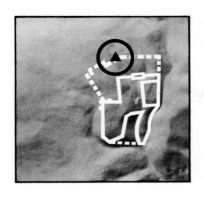

Pentecost

'When the day of Pentecost had come, they were all together in one place . . . And they were all filled with the Holy Spirit and began to speak in other tongues . . . Now there were in Jerusalem Jews, devout men from every nation under heaven. And at this sound the multitude came together, and they were bewildered, because each one heard them speaking in his own language . . .' Acts 2:1, 4-6

The medieval Damascus Gate in Jerusalem was the starting-point of the trade-route to Damascus in Syria. In New Testament times, too, Jerusalem was a cosmopolitan city with trade and religious links throughout the ancient world. The Feast of Pentecost brought together Jews from far and wide (see verses 9-11). The immediate result of the giving of the Holy Spirit was Peter's powerful address to this international gathering.

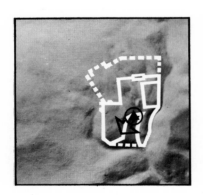

Persecution and outreach

'They cast him out of the city and stoned him . . . A great persecution arose against the church in Jerusalem; and they were all scattered throughout the region of Judea and Samaria, except the apostles. Devout men buried Stephen, and made great lamentation over him . . .' Acts 7:58; 8:1, 2

The communal life and fellowship of the church in Jerusalem was not left in peace for long. Stephen was the first martyr of the new faith. His death triggered off fresh persecution. But the immediate effect of this was to spread the gospel more widely. There was also another, longer term effect: the impact of Stephen's death on the mind of a young man named Saul.

Samaria

'Now when the apostles at Jerusalem heard that Samaria had received the word of God, they sent to them Peter and John . . . Now when they had testified and spoken the word of the Lord, they returned to Jerusalem, preaching the gospel to many villages of the Samaritans.' Acts 8:14, 25

The hill-country of Samaria, north from Jerusalem, and Judea, south from Jerusalem, were the first obvious starting-points for the outreach of the gospel. The village pictured here is near the ancient capital of Samaria. Orthodox Jews steered clear of the area for they despised the Samaritans: they were of mixed race, and held rival sacrifices. The early Christians, particularly Philip, 'proclaimed to them the Christ'.

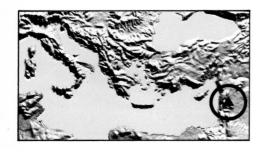

The road to Damascus

'But Saul, still breathing threats and murder against the disciples of the Lord, went to the high priest and asked for letters to the synagogues at Damascus, so that if he found any belonging to the Way, men or women, he might bring them bound to Jerusalem. Now as he journeyed he approached Damascus, and suddenly a light from heaven flashed about him . . .' Acts 9:1-3

Saul, who became the apostle Paul, was later to describe several times the dramatic events on the Damascus road. The risen Christ himself spoke unmistakably to him. In persecuting the church he had been persecuting Jesus himself. Saul fell to the ground. And when he rose he was blind, and had to be led by the hand into Damascus.

Paul was born in Tarsus, a large Romanized city and university town in what is now south-east Turkey. Pompey and Cicero were two famous Romans who had been involved in its government, and it was visited by Antony. Little remains from Roman times except this arch. But the fact that Paul was a Roman citizen was to be decisive in later events.

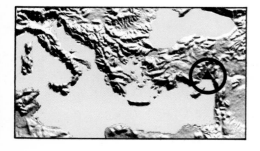

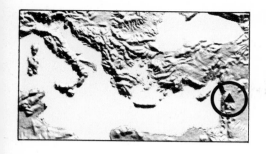

The Street called Straight

'Now there was a disciple at Damascus named Ananias. The Lord said to him in a vision, ". . . Rise and go to the street called Straight, and inquire in the house of Judas for a man of Tarsus named Saul; for behold, he is praying . . ."'
Acts 9:10, 11

The Street called Straight in Damascus is today a busy artery of the old covered markets. A Roman gateway at one end and ancient walls show what was once the extent of the city. Paul 'was without sight, and neither ate nor drank' for three days. His identification with his Lord's own death and resurrection to newness of life was then sealed as Ananias baptised him. It was in Damascus that he first preached, in the numerous synagogues; and on his return there later he had to escape by being lowered ignominiously down from a window in the city wall.

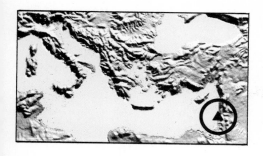

Joppa

'"Cornelius, . . . send men to Joppa, and bring one Simon who is called Peter; he is lodging with Simon, a tanner, whose house is by the seaside." . . . Peter went up on the housetop to pray, about the sixth hour. And he became hungry and desired something to eat; but while they were preparing it, he fell into a trance . . .' Acts 10:3f.

This flat roof in Jaffa has lattice-work as a shade against the sun. The equivalent at the house of Simon the tanner would have been an awning tied at the corners. In his trance Peter saw 'a great sheet' filled with creatures both 'clean' and 'unclean' by Jewish law. 'What God has cleansed', he was told, 'you must not call common.' The implications became clear when he visited Cornelius. The gospel was not only for Jews, but also for the Gentiles.

Antioch

'Barnabas went to Tarsus to look for Paul: and when he had found him, he brought him to Antioch. For a whole year they met with the church, and taught a large number of people; and in Antioch the disciples were for the first time called Christians.' Acts 11:25, 26

Antioch, on the River Orontes, was capital of the Roman province of Syria and the third largest city of the Empire. So it was perhaps natural that its Christian church should have been fast-growing and energetic. It sent money for famine relief to the church in Jerusalem. At Antioch 'overseas missions' were born when the church sent out Paul and Barnabas. The church challenged those in Jerusalem who insisted on Jewish traditions. The town is today called Antakya, in the south-eastern corner of Turkey near the border with Syria.

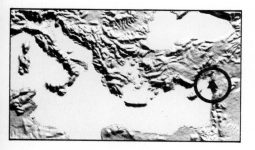

95

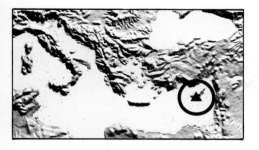

Cyprus

'While they were worshipping the Lord and fasting, the Holy Spirit said, "Set apart for me Barnabas and Saul for the work to which I have called them." . . . So, being sent out by the Holy Spirit, they went down to Seleucia; and from there they sailed to Cyprus. When they arrived at Salamis, they proclaimed the word of God . . .' Acts 13:2, 4, 5

Salamis was the first stop in this first missionary journey. Paul and Barnabas set the pattern for their work by preaching first in the Jewish synagogues. Salamis today consists of extensive ruins scattered over an area of sand-dune and woodland near Famagusta. The theatre, gymnasium (pictured here), harbour and other remains evoke something of the prosperous city which confronted the missionaries with all the power of a predominantly Roman culture.

aphos, at the other end of Cyprus, as where Paul met the proconsul ergius Paulus. The Roman ruins ictured here may have been the roconsul's residence; or remains f the forum.

Today extensive Roman, Hellenistic and Byzantine ruins surround the harbour from which Paul and Barnabas sailed for the next stage of their mission.

Pisidian Antioch

'Now Paul and his company set sail from Paphos and came to Perga in Pamphylia. And John (Mark) left them and returned to Jerusalem; but they passed on from Perga and came to Antioch of Pisidia. And on the sabbath day they went into the synagogue and sat down . . . Paul stood up, and motioning with his hand, said, "Men of Israel, and you that fear God, listen . . ."'
Acts 13:13-16

In making first for Perga (see page 105) and then Pisidian Antioch Paul pursued the same policy which later took him to Athens and Rome. He deliberately made for main centres from which the gospel would be taken to the surrounding district by the converts rather than the missionaries. Pisidian Antioch was a centre of Hellenistic Greek and Roman culture with a considerable Jewish settlement. High in what is now central Turkey, it had a magnificent setting. The Roman aqueducts pictured here once brought water to the city which now lies in ruins.

Lystra

'When the crowds saw what Paul had done, they lifted up their voices, saying in Lycaonian, "The gods have come down to us in the likeness of men!" Barnabas they called Zeus, and Paul, because he was the chief speaker, they called Hermes. And the priest of Zeus, whose temple was in front of the city, brought oxen and garlands to the gates and wanted to offer sacrifice with the people . . .' Acts 14:11-13

The setting of Lystra is a landscape of rocks, mountains and fertile plain. Faced, not now with Jews, but with superstitious pagans, the missionaries had to change their tactics. They started from God as Creator, 'the living God who made the heaven and the earth . . .' Today the nearby site of Lystra itself is no more than a litter of fallen stones.

Head of Hermes, found at Pergamum (Izmir Archaeological Museum)

Attalia

'And when they had spoken the word in Perga, they went down to Attalia; and from there they sailed to Antioch, where they had been commended to the grace of God for the work which they had fulfilled.' Acts 14:25, 26

A trading schooner lies in the small harbour of the modern resort town of Antalya, formerly Attalia, on the south coast of Turkey.

Extensive ruins remain at Perga, a short distance inland, which the missionaries visited on both their outward and return journeys.

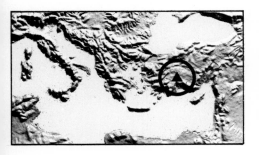

Pisidia

'And after some days Paul said to Barnabas, "Come, let us return and visit the brethren in every city where we proclaimed the word of the Lord, and see how they are."' Acts 15:36

The second missionary journey retraced the steps of the first before breaking new ground. Their route took them hundreds of miles across the mountains and plains of what is now central Turkey.

ΝΕΑ ΠΡΗΚΟΝΙΣΟΣ Ν.Χ. 91

Neapolis

'A vision appeared to Paul in the night: a man of Macedonia was standing beseeching him and saying, "Come over to Macedonia and help us." . . . Setting sail therefore from Troas, we made a direct voyage to Samothrace, and the following day to Neapolis . . .'
Acts 16: 9, 11

As the missionaries stepped ashore at Neapolis, modern Kavalla in northern Greece, they brought the gospel for the first time to Europe. Luke's account changes suddenly at Troas from 'they' to 'we'. Was he the man from Macedonia whose urgent requests for help gave Paul his night-time vision of the need 'to go on into Macedonia'?

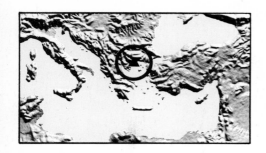

Philippi

'. . . And from there to Philippi, which is the leading city of the district of Macedonia, and a Roman colony. We remained in this city some days . . .'
Acts 16: 12

It was characteristic of Paul's tactics that he made for the leading city of the district. It may also have been Luke's own home-town. The official names translated as 'rulers' (verse 19), 'magistrates' (verse 20), 'police' (verse 35) are precise and reflect Philippi's civic pride in its status as a Roman colony. The picture is of the Forum, with the ruins of a Byzantine basilica behind. Several places nearby could have been the 'riverside' where there was a 'place of prayer' (some of the streams are now being drained in the interests of mosquito control and irrigation).

The road to Thessalonica

'Now when they had passed through Amphipolis and Apollonia, they came to Thessalonica, where there was a synagogue of the Jews. And Paul went in, as was his custom, and for three weeks he argued with them from the scriptures . . .' Acts 17: 1, 2

The Via Egnatia was the main east-west Roman road, linking the west coast of Greece with what is now Istanbul. The stone slabs worn into ruts by the wheels of the traffic were those on which Paul and his companions trod as they made for Thessalonica, then as now the most prominent city of the region.

Today Thessaloniki is the second largest city in Greece. In later Roman times the Via Egnatia passed under the Arch of Galerius pictured here. The street is still called by the same name.

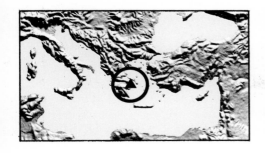

Athens

'Now while Paul was waiting for them at Athens, his spirit was provoked within him as he saw that the city was full of idols. So he argued in the synagogue with the Jews and the devout persons, and in the market place every day with those who chanced to be there . . . And they took hold of him and brought him to the Areopagus, saying, "May we know what this new teaching is which you present?" ' Acts 17: 16, 17, 19

Behind the agora, or market-place, at Athens rises the Acropolis (to the left), and Mars Hill, or the Areopagus (to the right). It was this hill which gave its name to the Council of the Areopagus which formerly met there. In Paul's day it met in one of the colonnaded buildings flanking the agora itself. It was before this learned body that Paul was taken to submit his 'new teaching'.

The Acropolis of Athens was a fortified sanctuary which was both the centre of its worship and its ultimate defensive position against invaders. The Parthenon, with which it is crowned, was built in the fifth century BC, the 'golden age' of Athens under Pericles. It has been successively a temple to the goddess Athena, a church, a mosque, a gunpowder store—and a shrine of classicism and tourism.

Corinth

'Many of the Corinthians hearing Paul believed and were baptized . . . And he stayed a year and six months, teaching the word of God among them. But when Gallio was proconsul of Achaia, the Jews made a united attack upon Paul and brought him before the tribunal . . .'
Acts 18: 8, 11, 12

The Temple of Apollo dominates the ancient site of Corinth today. Behind rises the fortress of Acro-Corinth. Near the temple the agora, or market-place, contains the remains of shops, temples, fountains, houses — and the 'bema', the official rostrum from which the Roman governor spoke. See too the picture on page 136.

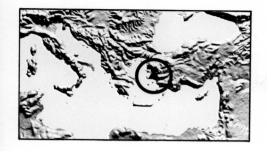

Ephesus: the temple

'. . . Not only at Ephesus but almost throughout all Asia this Paul has persuaded and turned away a considerable company of people, saying that gods made with hands are not gods. And there is danger not only that this trade of ours may come into disrepute but also that the temple of the great goddess Artemis may count for nothing, and that she may even be deposed from her magnificence, she whom all Asia and the world worship . . .' Acts 19: 26, 27

Demetrius and his fellow silversmiths found that the effects of the Christian gospel were threatening their trade in 'silver shrines of Artemis'. The great Temple of Artemis, or Diana, was one of the wonders of the ancient world. It is now a great rectangular area of marsh and water littered with broken pillars.

The nearby Museum of Ephesus contains two larger-than-life-size statues of the goddess. This one is a Roman version in white marble. Diana was the Roman goddess of chastity, Artemis the Greek goddess of love. It is typical of the place that the two were identified — and merged with the ancient local fertility cults.

Ephesus: the theatre

'. . . When they heard this they were enraged, and cried out, "Great is Artemis of the Ephesians!" So the city was filled with the confusion; and they rushed together into the theatre. . . . Now some cried one thing, some another; for the assembly was in confusion, and most of them did not know why they had come together . . .' Acts 19: 28, 32

The theatre is but one of the magnificent and extensive remains still being uncovered by archaeologists at Ephesus. The road leads down to what was once the harbour, long since silted up.

The main street at Ephesus. Hadrian's Temple (see page 140) is on the left.

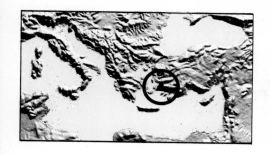

Miletus

'From Miletus he sent to Ephesus and called to him the elders of the church. And when they came to him, he said to them: "You yourselves know how I lived among you all the time from the first day that I set foot in Asia, serving the Lord with all humility and with tears and with trials . . . And now, behold, I am going to Jerusalem, bound in the Spirit, not knowing what shall befall me there . . .".'
Acts 20:17-19, 22

Miletus, 50 miles by road from Ephesus, was another of the great cosmopolitan cities of the west coast of Asia Minor, colonies of Hellenistic Greek culture. Like Ephesus, it boasts the remains of a magnificent theatre. Seat reservations are inscribed on the stone seats, including one for Jews and God-fearers.

Paul reminded the Ephesian elders at Miletus to look after their flock as shepherds protect their sheep from marauding wolves.

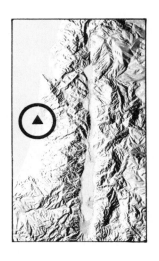

Caesarea

'So the soldiers, according to their instructions, took Paul and brought him by night to Antipatris. And on the morrow they returned to the barracks, leaving the horsemen to go on with him. When they came to Caesarea and delivered the letter to the governor, they presented Paul also before him.' Acts 23:31-33

Paul had already passed through Caesarea on his way to Jerusalem. He was brought back there ignominiously, under arrest and hurriedly removed from Jerusalem to save him from a Jewish plot. Caesarea was the centre of local Roman government — and Paul was a Roman citizen. The governor Felix heard his case; then left him in prison for two years. His successor, Festus, and the puppet king Herod Agrippa then listened to his defence. But Paul appealed to Caesar. Roman pillars are washed by the sea in what remains of Caesarea; they were used to strengthen Crusader walls.

Statues, a theatre, a horse-racing stadium, aqueduct, and remains of harbour breakwaters remain from Roman times. An inscription bearing the name of Pilate was unearthed in 1961.

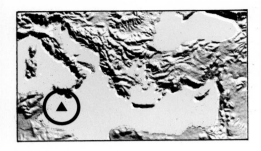

Malta

'Now when it was day, they did not recognize the land, but they noticed a bay with a beach, on which they planned if possible to bring the ship ashore . . . But striking a shoal they ran the vessel aground; the bow struck and remained immovable, and the stern was broken up by the surf . . . After we had escaped, we then learned that the island was called Malta.' Acts 27:39, 41; 28:1

Storm and shipwreck meant a three-month delay in the journey to Rome. St Paul's Bay, as it is called today, meets the conditions of the description in Acts precisely. A shallow sandbank runs out from the distant spit of land: it was this the ship struck while they were making for the beach beyond. Their misfortune was the island's fortune: many, including the governor's father, found healing through Paul's prayers.

The road to Rome

'And so we came to Rome. And the brethren there, when they heard of us, came as far as the Forum of Appius and Three Taverns to meet us. On seeing them Paul thanked God and took courage.' Acts 28:15

Outside Rome the ancient Roman road the Via Appia is lined with monuments. Stretches of original paving, rutted by cart-wheels, are still used by modern traffic.

Rome

'And he lived there two whole years at his own expense, and welcomed all who came to him, preaching the kingdom of God and teaching about the Lord Jesus Christ quite openly and unhindered.' Acts 28:30, 31

Paul had reached the heart of the ancient world. Whether or not he was able to fulfil his ambition to take the gospel to Spain, or whether he lived in Rome until the end of his days, we do not know. The Colosseum, the enormous amphitheatre built in AD 80, took its name from the colossal statue of Nero that stood near it. Here 45,000 spectators could watch fights between gladiators, even simulated naval battles. Here, when persecution later reached its height, Christians were thrown to lions to make sport for the crowds.

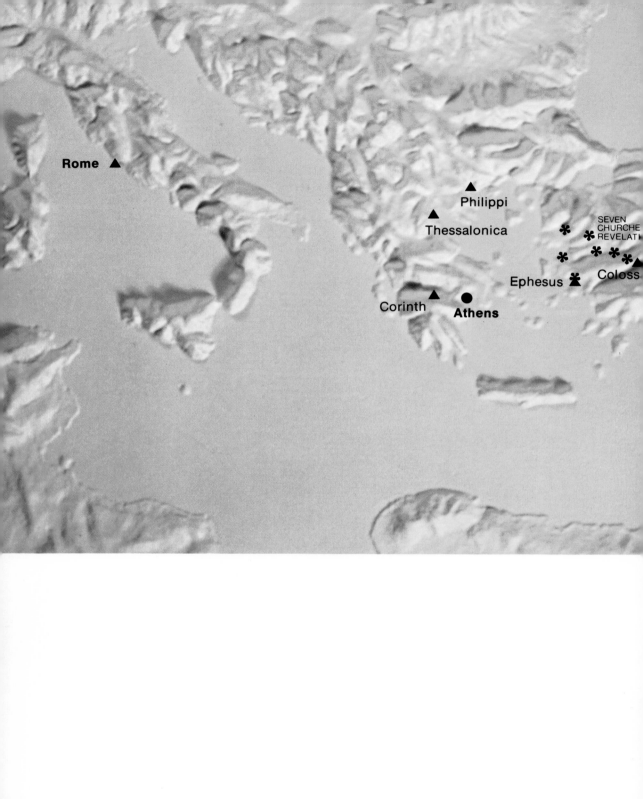

Rome ▲

Philippi ▲

Thessalonica ▲

✳ ✳ SEVEN
CHURCHE
REVELAT

✳ ✳ ✳ ✳

Corinth ▲   ● Athens

Ephesus ✳ Coloss

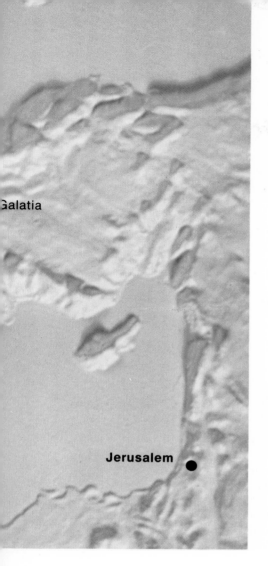

Galatia

Jerusalem ●

PART FOUR

Letters to the Churches

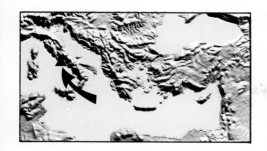

Romans

'Greet Prisca and Aquila, my fellow workers in Christ Jesus . . .; greet also the church in their house. Greet my beloved Epaenetus . . .' Romans 16:3-5

Paul has a considerable list of greetings at the end of his letter to the Christians at Rome. There were in the church people of rank, members of the imperial household, people from Greek and Roman and Jewish backgrounds. The Forum at Rome was the city centre with its main public buildings, and its principal meeting-place.

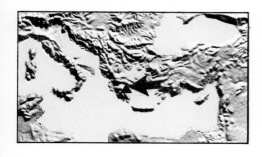

Corinthians

'For just as the body is one and has many members, and all the members of the body, though many, are one body, so it is with Christ. For by one Spirit we were all baptized into one body—Jews or Greek, slaves or free . . .'
1 Corinthians 12:12, 13

Corinth was an industrial and trading city with a proverbial reputation for immorality. It had road-links with harbours on both sides of the narrow isthmus: the Lechaion road in this picture led to the principal port. Many of the Corinthian church's problems arose from its particular situation: the party divisions reflected the town's mixed population; there was open immorality; meat sold in the market came from pagan sacrifices; women must be veiled to avoid suspicion of prostitution; there were extremes of emphasis on Greek philosophy, or on spiritual gifts associated with the mystery religions. (See also page 116.)

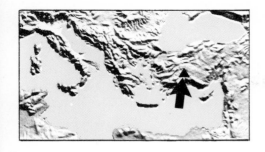

Galatians

'O foolish Galatians! Who has bewitched you, before whose eyes Jesus Christ was publicly portrayed as crucified? Let me ask you only this: Did you receive the Spirit by works of the law, or by hearing with faith?' Galatians 3:1, 2

It is a matter of debate whether Paul wrote to the Roman province of Galatia generally or the 'Galatian' or 'Gallic' people (settlers in the 3rd century BC) in the more northern part alone. But the purpose of the letter is clear: to prevent the churches giving in to Jewish elements who were denying the gospel by preaching 'salvation by law-keeping'. The picture is of a Jewish synagogue dating from the early centuries AD found at Sardis (one of the 'seven churches' of Revelation).

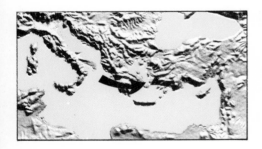

Ephesians

'So then you are . . . built upon the foundation of the apostles and prophets, Christ Jesus himself being the chief corner-stone, in whom the whole structure is joined together and grows into a holy temple in the Lord; in whom you also are built into it for a dwelling-place of God in the Spirit.' Ephesians 2:19-22

This Temple at Ephesus was dedicated to Hadrian, the Roman Emperor some years later than the time when this letter was written. It shows something of the splendour of the buildings of the time (see too page 120), and also illustrates the Emperor-worship which was to become a cause of persecution of the Christians for whom Jesus alone is Lord. At Smyrna, nearby, the aged Polycarp was to say before his martyrdom in AD 155, 'Eighty-six years have I served him, and he has done me no wrong; how then can I blaspheme my king who saved me?'

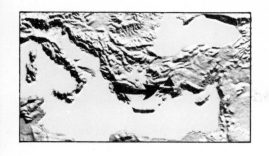

Colossians

'He is the image of the invisible God, the first-born of all creation; for in him all things are created . . .' Colossians 1:15, 16

Colossae was across a broad fertile valley from Laodicea and Hierapolis (see page 151). The mound of the ancient town, lying near the village of Honaz in the background of the picture, is yet to be excavated. Paul's letter was written to combat 'gnosticism'. Its combination of nature mysticism and speculations on created and uncreated beings would have appealed to a predominantly agricultural community in an area surrounded by mountains. As long ago as Heraclitus in the sixth century BC the people had been convinced that 'the world is full of spiritual beings'.

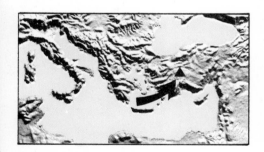

The Letters of Peter

'You have been born anew, not of perishable seed but of imperishable, through the living and abiding word of God: for "All flesh is like grass and all its glory like the flower of grass . . ."'
1 Peter 1:23, 24

Peter wrote to strengthen the Christians in what is now Turkey because of coming persecution and trials. In doing so he used vivid images they would appreciate: seedtime and harvest, flocks and shepherds, 'waterless springs and mists driven by a storm'.

Smyrna

'Write what you see in a book and send it to the seven churches, to Ephesus and to Smyrna and to Pergamum and to Thyatira and to Sardis and to Philadelphia and to Laodicea . . . Do not fear what you are about to suffer. Behold, the devil is about to throw some of you into prison, that you may be tested . . .'
Revelation 1:11; 2:10

The aged apostle John was exiled on the island of Patmos. The book of Revelation was written mainly in the literary form of apocalyptic, possibly to disguise its anti-Roman content, certainly because its rich imagery was the only way to convey his vision of the lordship of Christ in history. The first part is a series of letters to seven churches on the mainland, in the order in which a messenger would have reached them. Smyrna is today the busy industrial seaport city of Izmir. The Forum, pictured here, is the chief evidence of its Roman past.

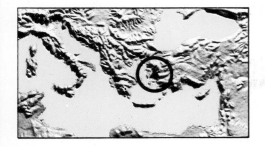

Pergamum

'I know where you dwell, where Satan's throne is . . .' Revelation 2:13

On a great rocky acropolis overlooking the small Turkish town of Bergama are the remains of the ancient town of Pergamum. Behind the theatre is the site of the great altar of Zeus. Pergamum was not only a centre for the worship of the traditional gods, Zeus, Dionysus and Athena, but the place where the worship of the Roman Emperor first took hold.

Temple dedicated to the Emperor Trajan.

Away from the main acropolis of Pergamum is the ruin of a Temple of Asclepius, the god of healing. Under the floor were water conduits; behind the arch is the end of a tunnel which may have been used for some sort of shock therapy for nervous disease. Medical treatment was mixed with mystery religion: its pagan immorality may underlie some of the references in John's letter.

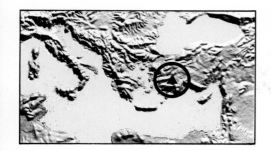

Laodicea

'I know your works: you are neither cold nor hot. Would that you were cold or hot! So, because you are lukewarm, and neither cold nor hot, I will spew you out of my mouth . . .' Revelation 3:15, 16

A few miles from Laodicea are the hot springs of Hierapolis. The two towns were mentioned together by Paul in his letter to Colossae, also nearby. The water was channelled along conduits to Laodicea itself — and would have arrived tepid.

Mineral deposits from the water onto the conduits have made them solid and permanent.

The waters from Hierapolis flow over cliffs: over the centuries the mineral deposits have built up into terraces and lime 'waterfalls'.

From the site of Laodicea itself the white cliffs of Hierapolis can be seen in the distance. Laodicea was also a commercial centre for banking and the wool trade, and a medical centre: gold, clothing and eye-salve are all alluded to in John's letter.

151

Judgment and glory

'Alas, alas for the great city . . . In one hour she has been laid waste. Rejoice over her, O heaven, O saints and apostles and prophets, for God has given judgment for you against her!' . . . I heard what seemed to be the voice of a great multitude . . . crying, 'Hallelujah! For the Lord our God the Almighty reigns. Let us rejoice and exult and give him the glory . . .' Revelation 18:19, 20; 19:6, 7

Revelation was written against the background of persecution and martyrdom, to encourage endurance to the end. It also looked to a time when even the persecuting Roman Empire itself would pass, when Christ and his faithful followers would be vindicated; when there would be new heavens and a new earth.